LEVEL UP

A Mindful Planner to Record Goals + Dreams

DOMINIQUE DEW

The Blue Foundation, LLC
ISBN: 978-1-7376366-0-1

A Mindful Planner to Record Goals + Dreams

PLAN LYFE THRU
A
NEW LENS

THIS PLANNER
BELONGS TO:

_____

By Dominique Dew

This Week

My Bills

- [ ] _____
- [ ] _____
- [ ] _____
- [ ] _____

My Leisure

- [ ] _____
- [ ] _____
- [ ] _____
- [ ] _____

My Total

- [ ] _____

Things To Do

- [ ] _____
- [ ] _____
- [ ] _____
- [ ] _____

Weekly Calendar

DATES_____

MONDAY

TUESDAY

WEDNESDAY

THURSDAY

FRIDAY

SATURDAY

SUNDAY

WORK HOURS STUDIES APPOINTMENT

This Week

My Bills

- [ ] _____
- [ ] _____
- [ ] _____
- [ ] _____

My Leisure

- [ ] _____
- [ ] _____
- [ ] _____
- [ ] _____

My Total

- [ ] _____

Things To Do

- [ ] _____
- [ ] _____
- [ ] _____
- [ ] _____

Weekly Calendar

DATES_____

MONDAY

TUESDAY

WEDNESDAY

THURSDAY

FRIDAY

SATURDAY

SUNDAY

WORK HOURS   STUDIES   APPOINTMENT

This Week

My Bills

- [ ] ....
- [ ] ....
- [ ] ....
- [ ] ....

My Leisure

- [ ] ....
- [ ] ....
- [ ] ....
- [ ] ....

My Total

- [ ] ....

Things To Do

- [ ] _____
- [ ] _____
- [ ] _____
- [ ] _____

Weekly Calendar

DATES_____

MONDAY

TUESDAY

WEDNESDAY

THURSDAY

FRIDAY

SATURDAY

SUNDAY

🪙 WORK HOURS   📖 STUDIES   📅 APPOINTMENT

This Week

My Bills

- [ ] _____
- [ ] _____
- [ ] _____
- [ ] _____

My Leisure

- [ ] _____
- [ ] _____
- [ ] _____
- [ ] _____

My Total

- [ ] _____

Things To Do

- [ ] _____
- [ ] _____
- [ ] _____
- [ ] _____

Weekly Calendar

DATES _____

MONDAY

TUESDAY

WEDNESDAY

THURSDAY

FRIDAY

SATURDAY

SUNDAY

WORK HOURS   STUDIES   APPOINTMENT

"All your dreams can come true if you have the courage to pursue them"
-Walt Disney

MONTHLY BUDGET

	INCOME	
Pay Date	Income Source	Amount Earned
	Totals	

	EXPENSES	
Due Date	Expense	Amount Spent
	Totals	

DEPOSIT OF DREAMS

Money Not Spent:

Planned Savings:

$

This Week

My Bills

- [ ] _____
- [ ] _____
- [ ] _____
- [ ] _____

My Leisure

- [ ] _____
- [ ] _____
- [ ] _____
- [ ] _____

My Total

- [ ] _____

Things To Do

- [ ] _____
- [ ] _____
- [ ] _____
- [ ] _____

Weekly Calendar

DATES _____

MONDAY

TUESDAY

WEDNESDAY

THURSDAY

FRIDAY

SATURDAY

SUNDAY

WORK HOURS   STUDIES   APPOINTMENT

This Week

My Bills

- [ ] _____
- [ ] _____
- [ ] _____
- [ ] _____

My Leisure

- [ ] _____
- [ ] _____
- [ ] _____
- [ ] _____

My Total

- [ ] _____

Things To Do

- [ ] _____
- [ ] _____
- [ ] _____
- [ ] _____

Weekly Calendar

DATES _____

MONDAY

TUESDAY

WEDNESDAY

THURSDAY

FRIDAY

SATURDAY

SUNDAY

WORK HOURS STUDIES APPOINTMENT

This Week

My Bills

- [ ] _____
- [ ] _____
- [ ] _____
- [ ] _____

My Leisure

- [ ] _____
- [ ] _____
- [ ] _____
- [ ] _____

My Total

- [ ] _____

Things To Do

- [ ] _____
- [ ] _____
- [ ] _____
- [ ] _____

Weekly Calendar

DATES_____

MONDAY

TUESDAY

WEDNESDAY

THURSDAY

FRIDAY

SATURDAY

SUNDAY

WORK HOURS STUDIES APPOINTMENT

This Week

My Bills

- [ ] ....
- [ ] ....
- [ ] ....
- [ ] ....

My Leisure

- [ ] ....
- [ ] ....
- [ ] ....
- [ ] ....

My Total

- [ ] ....

Things To Do

- [ ] ....
- [ ] ....
- [ ] ....
- [ ] ....

Weekly Calendar

DATES_____

MONDAY

TUESDAY

WEDNESDAY

THURSDAY

FRIDAY

SATURDAY

SUNDAY

WORK HOURS   STUDIES   APPOINTMENT

Everyone won't see your vision so if it's different from what others are doing that's a great thing!

MONTHLY BUDGET

INCOME

Pay Date	Income Source	Amount Earned
	Totals	

EXPENSES

Due Date	Expense	Amount Spent
	Totals	

DEPOSIT OF DREAMS

Money Not Spent:

Planned Savings:

do. be. have

Write it down and see just how real it gets

Create your goals

GOALS:

PLAN OF ACTION:

PROJECTED DATE:

EDUCATION

GOALS:

PLAN OF ACTION:

PROJECTED DATE:

CAREER

pray. love. make $$

Write it down and see just how real it gets

Create your goals

GOALS:

PLAN OF ACTION:

PROJECTED DATE:

LIVING SPACE

MILESTONES:

THINGS THAT WORKED:

THINGS THAT I COULD DO BETTER:

REFLECTIONS

This Week

My Bills

- [ ] _____
- [ ] _____
- [ ] _____
- [ ] _____

My Leisure

- [ ] _____
- [ ] _____
- [ ] _____
- [ ] _____

My Total

- [ ] _____

Things To Do

- [ ] _____
- [ ] _____
- [ ] _____
- [ ] _____

Weekly Calendar

DATES_____

MONDAY

TUESDAY

WEDNESDAY

THURSDAY

FRIDAY

SATURDAY

SUNDAY

WORK HOURS   STUDIES   APPOINTMENT

This Week

My Bills

- ☐ ....
- ☐ ....
- ☐ ....
- ☐ ....

My Leisure

- ☐ ....
- ☐ ....
- ☐ ....
- ☐ ....

My Total

- ☐ ....

Things To Do

- ☐ ....
- ☐ ....

- ☐ ....
- ☐ ....

Weekly Calendar

DATES_____

MONDAY

TUESDAY

WEDNESDAY

THURSDAY

FRIDAY

SATURDAY

SUNDAY

WORK HOURS   STUDIES   APPOINTMENT

This Week

My Bills

- ☐ ....
- ☐ ....
- ☐ ....
- ☐ ....

My Leisure

- ☐ ....
- ☐ ....
- ☐ ....
- ☐ ....

My Total

- ☐ ....

Things To Do

- ☐ ....
- ☐ ....
- ☐ ....
- ☐ ....

Weekly Calendar

DATES_____

MONDAY
TUESDAY
WEDNESDAY

THURSDAY
FRIDAY
SATURDAY

SUNDAY

WORK HOURS STUDIES APPOINTMENT

This Week

My Bills

- [ ] _____
- [ ] _____
- [ ] _____
- [ ] _____

My Leisure

- [ ] _____
- [ ] _____
- [ ] _____
- [ ] _____

My Total

- [ ] _____

Things To Do

- [ ] _____
- [ ] _____
- [ ] _____
- [ ] _____

Weekly Calendar

DATES _____

MONDAY

TUESDAY

WEDNESDAY

THURSDAY

FRIDAY

SATURDAY

SUNDAY

WORK HOURS   STUDIES   APPOINTMENT

MONTHLY BUDGET

INCOME		
Pay Date	**Income Source**	**Amount Earned**
	Totals	

EXPENSES		
Due Date	**Expense**	**Amount Spent**
	Totals	

DEPOSIT OF DREAMS		

Money Not Spent:

Planned Savings:

This Week

My Bills

- [ ] _____
- [ ] _____
- [ ] _____
- [ ] _____

My Leisure

- [ ] _____
- [ ] _____
- [ ] _____
- [ ] _____

My Total

- [ ] _____

Things To Do

- [ ] _____
- [ ] _____
- [ ] _____
- [ ] _____

Weekly Calendar

DATES_____

MONDAY

TUESDAY

WEDNESDAY

THURSDAY

FRIDAY

SATURDAY

SUNDAY

WORK HOURS   STUDIES   APPOINTMENT

This Week

My Bills

- [ ] _____
- [ ] _____
- [ ] _____
- [ ] _____

My Leisure

- [ ] _____
- [ ] _____
- [ ] _____
- [ ] _____

My Total

- [ ] _____

Things To Do

- [ ] _____
- [ ] _____

- [ ] _____
- [ ] _____

Weekly Calendar

DATES_____

MONDAY

TUESDAY

WEDNESDAY

THURSDAY

FRIDAY

SATURDAY

SUNDAY

WORK HOURS

STUDIES

APPOINTMENT

This Week

My Bills

- [ ] _____
- [ ] _____
- [ ] _____
- [ ] _____

My Leisure

- [ ] _____
- [ ] _____
- [ ] _____
- [ ] _____

My Total

- [ ] _____

Things To Do

- [ ] _____
- [ ] _____
- [ ] _____
- [ ] _____

Weekly Calendar

DATES _____

MONDAY

TUESDAY

WEDNESDAY

THURSDAY

FRIDAY

SATURDAY

SUNDAY

WORK HOURS   STUDIES   APPOINTMENT

This Week

My Bills

- [ ] ....
- [ ] ....
- [ ] ....
- [ ] ....

My Leisure

- [ ] ....
- [ ] ....
- [ ] ....
- [ ] ....

My Total

- [ ] ....

Things To Do

- [ ] ....
- [ ] ....
- [ ] ....
- [ ] ....

Weekly Calendar

DATES_____

MONDAY

TUESDAY

WEDNESDAY

THURSDAY

FRIDAY

SATURDAY

SUNDAY

WORK HOURS   STUDIES   APPOINTMENT

DREAM CHASE
Remove all the **ne**g**a**tive thoughts; a**ppro**ach **your** next **steps** in li**fe** with **p**atienc**e, positiv**ty and a **stro**ng belief in **G**od's **p**lan

MONTHLY BUDGET

INCOME

Pay Date	Income Source	Amount Earned
	Totals	

EXPENSES

Due Date	Expense	Amount Spent
	Totals	

DEPOSIT OF DREAMS

Money Not Spent:

Planned Savings:

This Week

My Bills

- [ ] _____
- [ ] _____
- [ ] _____
- [ ] _____

My Leisure

- [ ] _____
- [ ] _____
- [ ] _____
- [ ] _____

My Total

- [ ] _____

Things To Do

- [ ] _____   - [ ] _____
- [ ] _____   - [ ] _____

Weekly Calendar

DATES_____

MONDAY

TUESDAY

WEDNESDAY

THURSDAY

FRIDAY

SATURDAY

SUNDAY

WORK HOURS   STUDIES   APPOINTMENT

This Week

My Bills

- [ ] _____
- [ ] _____
- [ ] _____
- [ ] _____

My Leisure

- [ ] _____
- [ ] _____
- [ ] _____
- [ ] _____

My Total

- [ ] _____

Things To Do

- [ ] _____
- [ ] _____
- [ ] _____
- [ ] _____

Weekly Calendar

DATES_____

MONDAY

TUESDAY

WEDNESDAY

THURSDAY

FRIDAY

SATURDAY

SUNDAY

WORK HOURS   STUDIES   APPOINTMENT

This Week

My Bills

- [ ] _____
- [ ] _____
- [ ] _____
- [ ] _____

My Leisure

- [ ] _____
- [ ] _____
- [ ] _____
- [ ] _____

My Total

- [ ] _____

Things To Do

- [ ] _____
- [ ] _____
- [ ] _____
- [ ] _____

Weekly Calendar

DATES _____

MONDAY

TUESDAY

WEDNESDAY

THURSDAY

FRIDAY

SATURDAY

SUNDAY

WORK HOURS   STUDIES   APPOINTMENT

This Week

My Bills

- [ ] _____
- [ ] _____
- [ ] _____
- [ ] _____

My Leisure

- [ ] _____
- [ ] _____
- [ ] _____
- [ ] _____

My Total

- [ ] _____

Things To Do

- [ ] _____
- [ ] _____
- [ ] _____
- [ ] _____

Weekly Calendar

DATES_____

MONDAY

TUESDAY

WEDNESDAY

THURSDAY

FRIDAY

SATURDAY

SUNDAY

WORK HOURS STUDIES APPOINTMENT

LYFE IS LIKE A
CAMERA
FOCUS ON WHAT IS
IMPORTANT
CAPTURE THE GOOD
TIMES
DEVELOP FROM THE
NEGATIVE
IF THINGS DON'T WORK
OUT TAKE ANOTHER
SHOT

MONTHLY BUDGET

INCOME

Pay Date	Income Source	Amount Earned
	Totals	

EXPENSES

Due Date	Expense	Amount Spent
	Totals	

DEPOSIT OF DREAMS

Money Not Spent:

Planned Savings:

This Week

My Bills

- ☐ ....
- ☐ ....
- ☐ ....
- ☐ ....

My Leisure

- ☐ ....
- ☐ ....
- ☐ ....
- ☐ ....

My Total

- ☐ ....

Things To Do

- ☐ ....
- ☐ ....
- ☐ ....
- ☐ ....

Weekly Calendar

DATES _____

MONDAY

TUESDAY

WEDNESDAY

THURSDAY

FRIDAY

SATURDAY

SUNDAY

WORK HOURS   STUDIES   APPOINTMENT

This Week

My Bills

- [ ] _____
- [ ] _____
- [ ] _____
- [ ] _____

My Leisure

- [ ] _____
- [ ] _____
- [ ] _____
- [ ] _____

My Total

- [ ] _____

Things To Do

- [ ] _____
- [ ] _____
- [ ] _____
- [ ] _____

Weekly Calendar

DATES_____

MONDAY

TUESDAY

WEDNESDAY

THURSDAY

FRIDAY

SATURDAY

SUNDAY

WORK HOURS   STUDIES   APPOINTMENT

This Week

My Bills

- [ ] _____
- [ ] _____
- [ ] _____
- [ ] _____

My Leisure

- [ ] _____
- [ ] _____
- [ ] _____
- [ ] _____

My Total

- [ ] _____

Things To Do

- [ ] _____
- [ ] _____
- [ ] _____
- [ ] _____

Weekly Calendar

DATES_____

MONDAY

TUESDAY

WEDNESDAY

THURSDAY

FRIDAY

SATURDAY

SUNDAY

WORK HOURS   STUDIES   APPOINTMENT

This Week

My Bills

- [ ] ....
- [ ] ....
- [ ] ....
- [ ] ....

My Leisure

- [ ] ....
- [ ] ....
- [ ] ....
- [ ] ....

My Total

- [ ] ....

Things To Do

- [ ] ....
- [ ] ....
- [ ] ....
- [ ] ....

Weekly Calendar

MONDAY

TUESDAY

WEDNESDAY

THURSDAY

FRIDAY

SATURDAY

SUNDAY

WORK HOURS   STUDIES   APPOINTMENT

DECIDE WHAT YOU WANT

DECIDE WHAT YOU ARE

WILLING TO EXCHANGE FOR IT

ESTABLISH YOUR PRIORITIES

AND GO 2 WORK

MONTHLY BUDGET

INCOME		
Pay Date	Income Source	Amount Earned
	Totals	

EXPENSES		
Due Date	Expense	Amount Spent
	Totals	

DEPOSIT OF DREAMS

Money Not Spent:

Planned Savings:

do. be. have
Write it down and see just how real it gets
Create your goals

Goals:

Plan of action:

Projecte Date:

EDUCATION

Goals:

Plan of action:

Projected Date:

CAREER

pray. love. make $$

Write it down and see just how real it gets

Create your goals

GOALS:

PLAN OF ACTION:

PROJECTED DATE:

LIVING SPACE

MILESTONES:

THINGS THAT WORKED:

THINGS THAT I COULD DO BETTER:

REFLECTIONS

This Week

My Bills

- [ ] _____
- [ ] _____
- [ ] _____
- [ ] _____

My Leisure

- [ ] _____
- [ ] _____
- [ ] _____
- [ ] _____

My Total

- [ ] _____

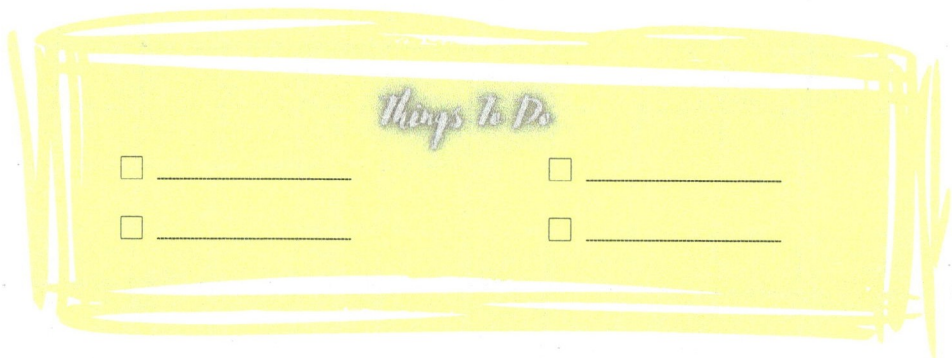

Things To Do

- [ ] _____
- [ ] _____
- [ ] _____
- [ ] _____

Weekly Calendar

DATES_____

MONDAY

TUESDAY

WEDNESDAY

THURSDAY

FRIDAY

SATURDAY

SUNDAY

WORK HOURS   STUDIES   APPOINTMENT

This Week

My Bills

- [ ] _____
- [ ] _____
- [ ] _____
- [ ] _____

My Leisure

- [ ] _____
- [ ] _____
- [ ] _____
- [ ] _____

My Total

- [ ] _____

Things To Do

- [ ] _____
- [ ] _____
- [ ] _____
- [ ] _____

Weekly Calendar

DATES_____

MONDAY

TUESDAY

WEDNESDAY

THURSDAY

FRIDAY

SATURDAY

SUNDAY

🧺 WORK HOURS　　📖 STUDIES　　📅 APPOINTMENT

This Week

My Bills

- [ ] _____
- [ ] _____
- [ ] _____
- [ ] _____

My Leisure

- [ ] _____
- [ ] _____
- [ ] _____
- [ ] _____

My Total

- [ ] _____

Things To Do

- [ ] _____
- [ ] _____
- [ ] _____
- [ ] _____

Weekly Calendar

MONDAY

TUESDAY

WEDNESDAY

THURSDAY

FRIDAY

SATURDAY

SUNDAY

WORK HOURS   STUDIES   APPOINTMENT

This Week

My Bills

- [ ] _____
- [ ] _____
- [ ] _____
- [ ] _____

My Leisure

- [ ] _____
- [ ] _____
- [ ] _____
- [ ] _____

My Total

- [ ] _____

Things To Do

- [ ] _____
- [ ] _____
- [ ] _____
- [ ] _____

Weekly Calendar

DATES _____

MONDAY

TUESDAY

WEDNESDAY

THURSDAY

FRIDAY

SATURDAY

SUNDAY

WORK HOURS   STUDIES   APPOINTMENT

ONE YEAR FROM
NOW YOU WILL
WISH YOU HAD
STARTED TODAY
-KAREN LAMB

MONTHLY BUDGET

INCOME

Pay Date	Income Source	Amount Earned
	Totals	

EXPENSES

Due Date	Expense	Amount Spent
	Totals	

DEPOSIT OF DREAMS

Money Not Spent:

Planned Savings:

This Week

My Bills

- [ ] _____
- [ ] _____
- [ ] _____
- [ ] _____

My Leisure

- [ ] _____
- [ ] _____
- [ ] _____
- [ ] _____

My Total

- [ ] _____

Things To Do

- [ ] _____
- [ ] _____
- [ ] _____
- [ ] _____

Weekly Calendar

DATES_____

MONDAY

TUESDAY

WEDNESDAY

THURSDAY

FRIDAY

SATURDAY

SUNDAY

🛍️ WORK HOURS   📖 STUDIES   📅 APPOINTMENT

This Week

My Bills

- [ ] ....
- [ ] ....
- [ ] ....
- [ ] ....

My Leisure

- [ ] ....
- [ ] ....
- [ ] ....
- [ ] ....

My Total

- [ ] ....

Things To Do

- [ ] ....
- [ ] ....
- [ ] ....
- [ ] ....

Weekly Calendar

DATES_____

MONDAY

TUESDAY

WEDNESDAY

THURSDAY

FRIDAY

SATURDAY

SUNDAY

WORK HOURS   STUDIES   APPOINTMENT

This Week

My Bills

- [ ] _____
- [ ] _____
- [ ] _____
- [ ] _____

My Leisure

- [ ] _____
- [ ] _____
- [ ] _____
- [ ] _____

My Total

- [ ] _____

Things To Do

- [ ] _____
- [ ] _____
- [ ] _____
- [ ] _____

Weekly Calendar

DATES _____

MONDAY

TUESDAY

WEDNESDAY

THURSDAY

FRIDAY

SATURDAY

SUNDAY

WORK HOURS   STUDIES   APPOINTMENT

This Week

My Bills

- [ ] _____
- [ ] _____
- [ ] _____
- [ ] _____

My Leisure

- [ ] _____
- [ ] _____
- [ ] _____
- [ ] _____

My Total

- [ ] _____

Things To Do

- [ ] _____
- [ ] _____
- [ ] _____
- [ ] _____

Weekly Calendar

DATES_____

MONDAY

TUESDAY

WEDNESDAY

THURSDAY

FRIDAY

SATURDAY

SUNDAY

WORK HOURS   STUDIES   APPOINTMENT

LET GO
&
BE

MONTHLY BUDGET

INCOME

Pay Date	Income Source	Amount Earned
	Totals	

EXPENSES

Due Date	Expense	Amount Spent
	Totals	

DEPOSIT OF DREAMS

Money Not Spent:

Planned Savings:

This Week

My Bills

- [ ] _____
- [ ] _____
- [ ] _____
- [ ] _____

My Leisure

- [ ] _____
- [ ] _____
- [ ] _____
- [ ] _____

My Total

- [ ] _____

Things To Do

- [ ] _____
- [ ] _____

- [ ] _____
- [ ] _____

Weekly Calendar

DATES _____

MONDAY

TUESDAY

WEDNESDAY

THURSDAY

FRIDAY

SATURDAY

SUNDAY

WORK HOURS   STUDIES   APPOINTMENT

This Week

My Bills

- [ ] ....
- [ ] ....
- [ ] ....
- [ ] ....

My Leisure

- [ ] ....
- [ ] ....
- [ ] ....
- [ ] ....

My Total

- [ ] ....

Things To Do

- [ ] ....
- [ ] ....
- [ ] ....
- [ ] ....

Weekly Calendar

DATES_____

MONDAY

TUESDAY

WEDNESDAY

THURSDAY

FRIDAY

SATURDAY

SUNDAY

WORK HOURS   STUDIES   APPOINTMENT

This Week

My Bills

- [ ] _____
- [ ] _____
- [ ] _____
- [ ] _____

My Leisure

- [ ] _____
- [ ] _____
- [ ] _____
- [ ] _____

My Total

- [ ] _____

Things To Do

- [ ] _____
- [ ] _____
- [ ] _____
- [ ] _____

Weekly Calendar

DATES_____

MONDAY

TUESDAY

WEDNESDAY

THURSDAY

FRIDAY

SATURDAY

SUNDAY

WORK HOURS   STUDIES   APPOINTMENT

This Week

My Bills

- [ ] ....
- [ ] ....
- [ ] ....
- [ ] ....

My Leisure

- [ ] ....
- [ ] ....
- [ ] ....
- [ ] ....

My Total

- [ ] ....

Things To Do

- [ ] ....
- [ ] ....
- [ ] ....
- [ ] ....

Weekly Calendar

DATES _____

MONDAY

TUESDAY

WEDNESDAY

THURSDAY

FRIDAY

SATURDAY

SUNDAY

WORK HOURS   STUDIES   APPOINTMENT

IT'S ALL GOOD

BELIEVE DAT

MONTHLY BUDGET

INCOME

Pay Date	Income Source	Amount Earned
	Totals	

EXPENSES

Due Date	Expense	Amount Spent
	Totals	

DEPOSIT OF DREAMS

Money Not Spent:

Planned Savings:

do. be. have

Write it down and see just how real it gets

Create your goals

GOALS:

PLAN OF ACTION:

PROJECTED DATE:

EDUCATION

GOALS:

PLAN OF ACTION:

PROJECTED DATE:

CAREER

pray. love. make $$

Write it down and see just how real it gets

Create your goals

GOALS:

PLAN OF ACTION:

PROJECTED DATE:

LIVING SPACE

MILESTONES:

THINGS THAT WORKED:

THINGS THAT I COULD DO BETTER:

REFLECTIONS

www.ingramcontent.com/pod-product-compliance
Lightning Source LLC
LaVergne TN
LVHW010309070426
835511LV00021B/3456